BAREFOOT EMPRESS

STORY VIKAS KHANNA
ILLUSTRATIONS AARYAMA SOMAYAJI

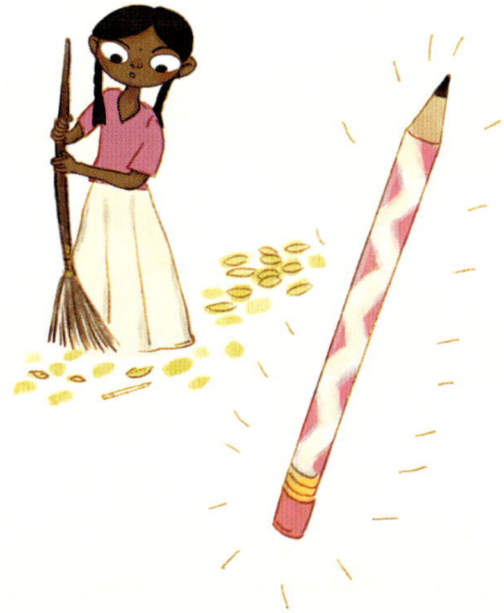

BLOOMSBURY
NEW DELHI • LONDON • OXFORD • NEW YORK • SYDNEY

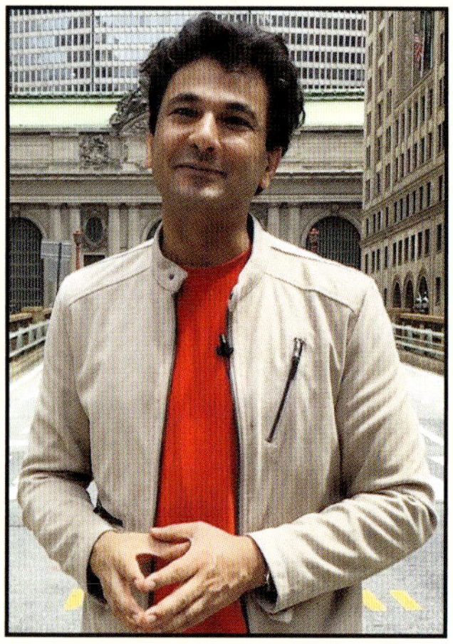

VIKAS KHANNA is an internationally acclaimed Indian American chef, film-maker and author. He is a James Beard nominee and one of the first Indian chefs to be awarded a Michelin Star for his restaurant in the US.

He has been featured among the ten most influential chefs in the world by Deutsche Welle and Gazette Review. He is the host of *MasterChef India*, *Twist of Taste* and *India's Megakitchens* on National Geographic. Khanna is the author of 38 books, including *Utsav: A Culinary Epic of Indian Festivals* (world's most expensive cookbook) and the creator of the documentary series *Holy Kitchens* and *Kitchens of Gratitude*.

He founded the Museum of Kitchen Arts, which is home to thousands of India's unique kitchen tools and equipment, at his alma mater, WGSHA, Manipal, India.

His restaurants, Kinara and Ellora, are rated as Dubai's favourite Indian restaurants by *Condé Nast*.

His initiative Feed India served more than 51 million meals during the Covid-19 pandemic. *The Last Color*, which was considered for the best feature film award at the 2020 Academy Awards, marked Khanna's debut as a film writer and director.

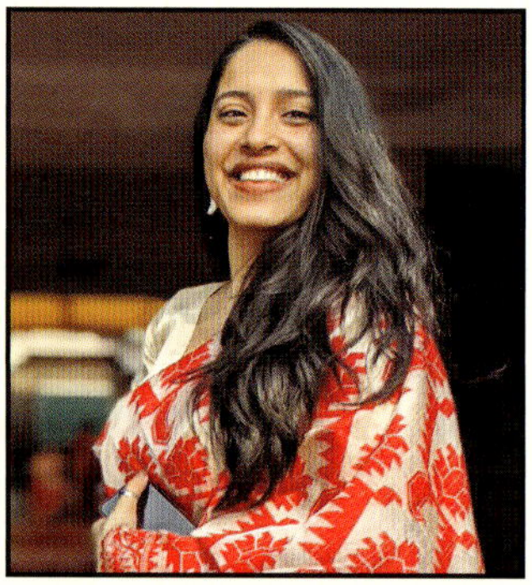

AARYAMA SOMAYAJI studied communication design at National Institute of Design, Andhra Pradesh. She is a freelance illustrator and book cover designer. Besides publishing, her projects include branding and packaging for food brands. She draws to survive, reads for herself and eats to stay happy. Her work can be found on www.instagram.com/highonmangoes.

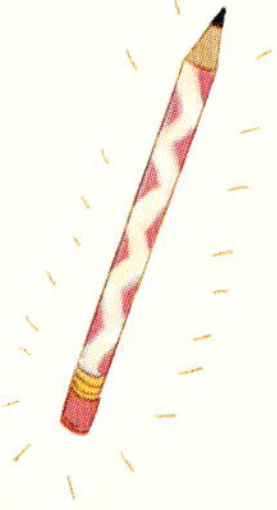

For my sister Radhika.
Thank you for being the
inspiration to educate
the girl child

And celebrating the birth of
Luiza Fonseca Roland

– Vikas Khanna

To Appa,
all children should have
teachers like you!

– Aaryama Somayaji

In 1922, a little girl was born in a village in Kerala. She had sparkling eyes like Ma Durga and was named Karthyayani. She loved sunlight, flowers, jackfruit and books. She dreamed of going to school one day.

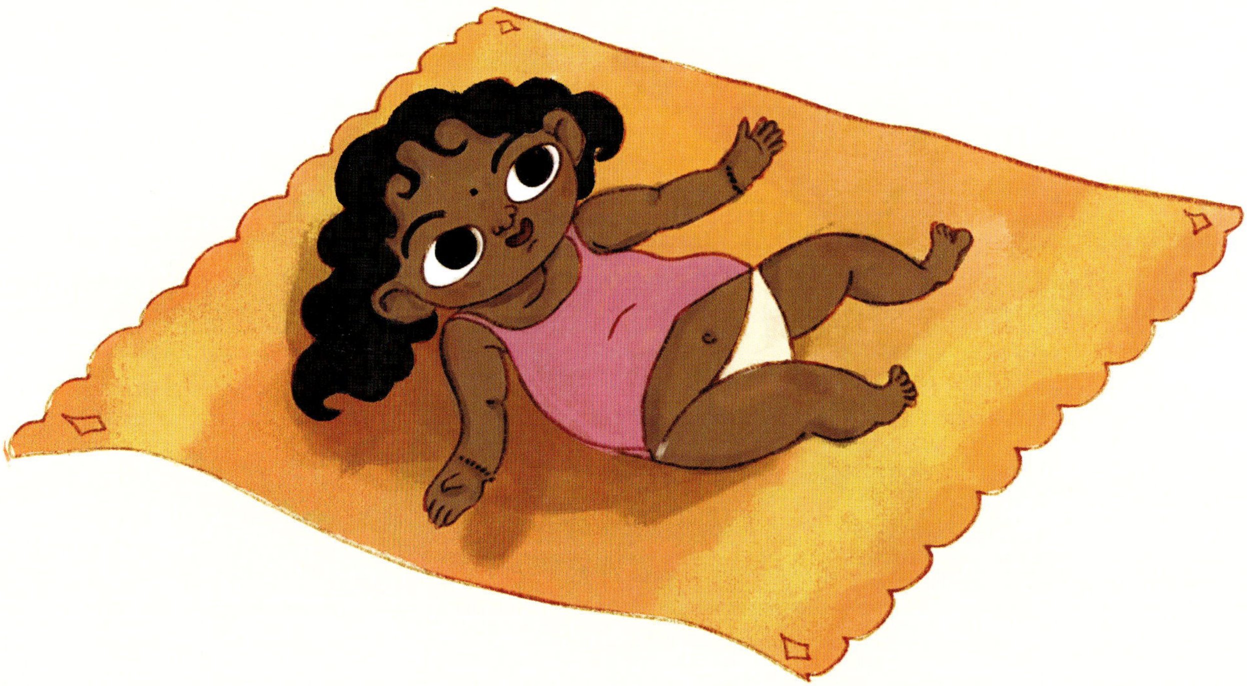

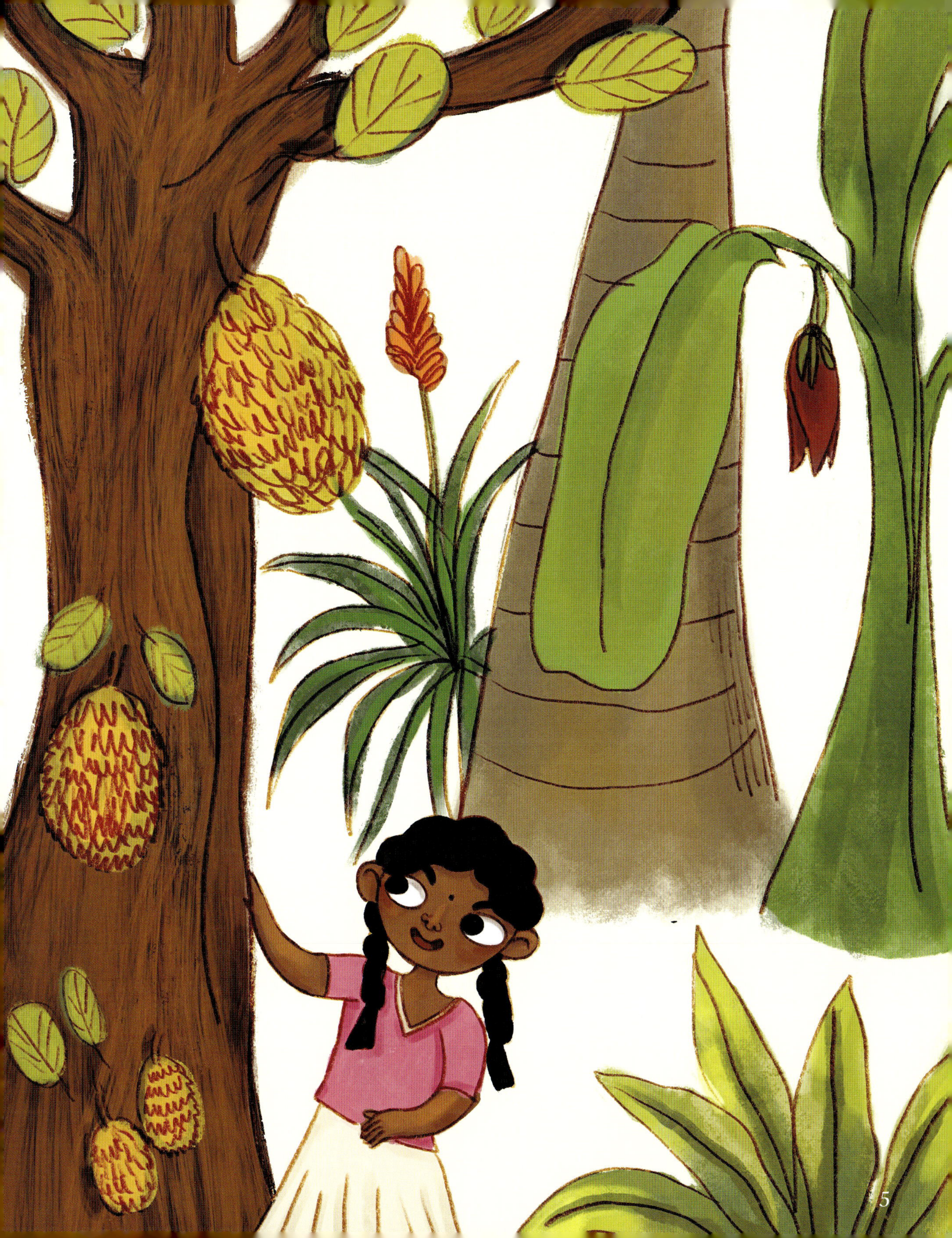

Some days she would stand in front of the mirror and pretend she was sitting in a classroom. One day, she found a pink-and-white pencil outside a temple. She saved it to use in school.

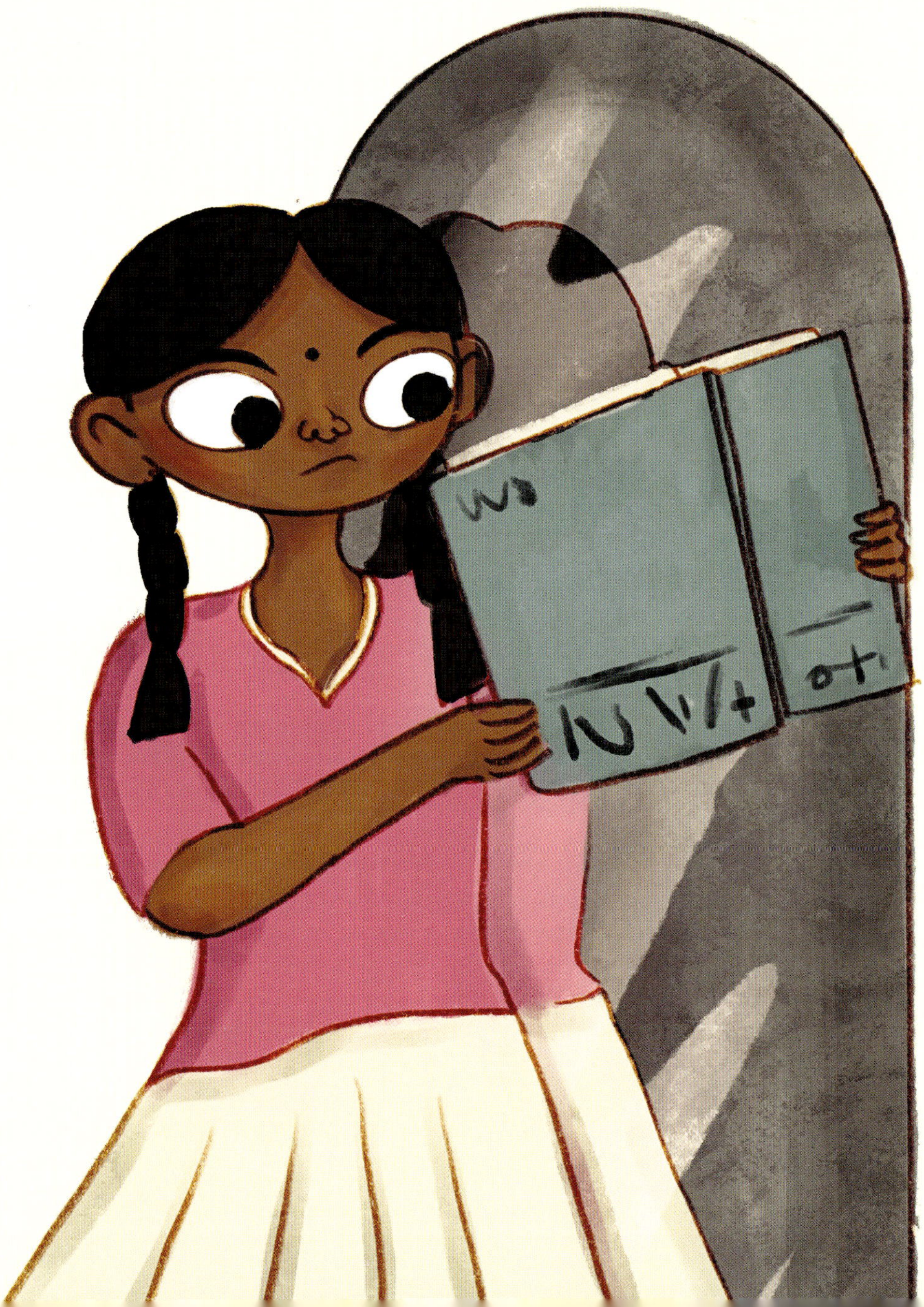

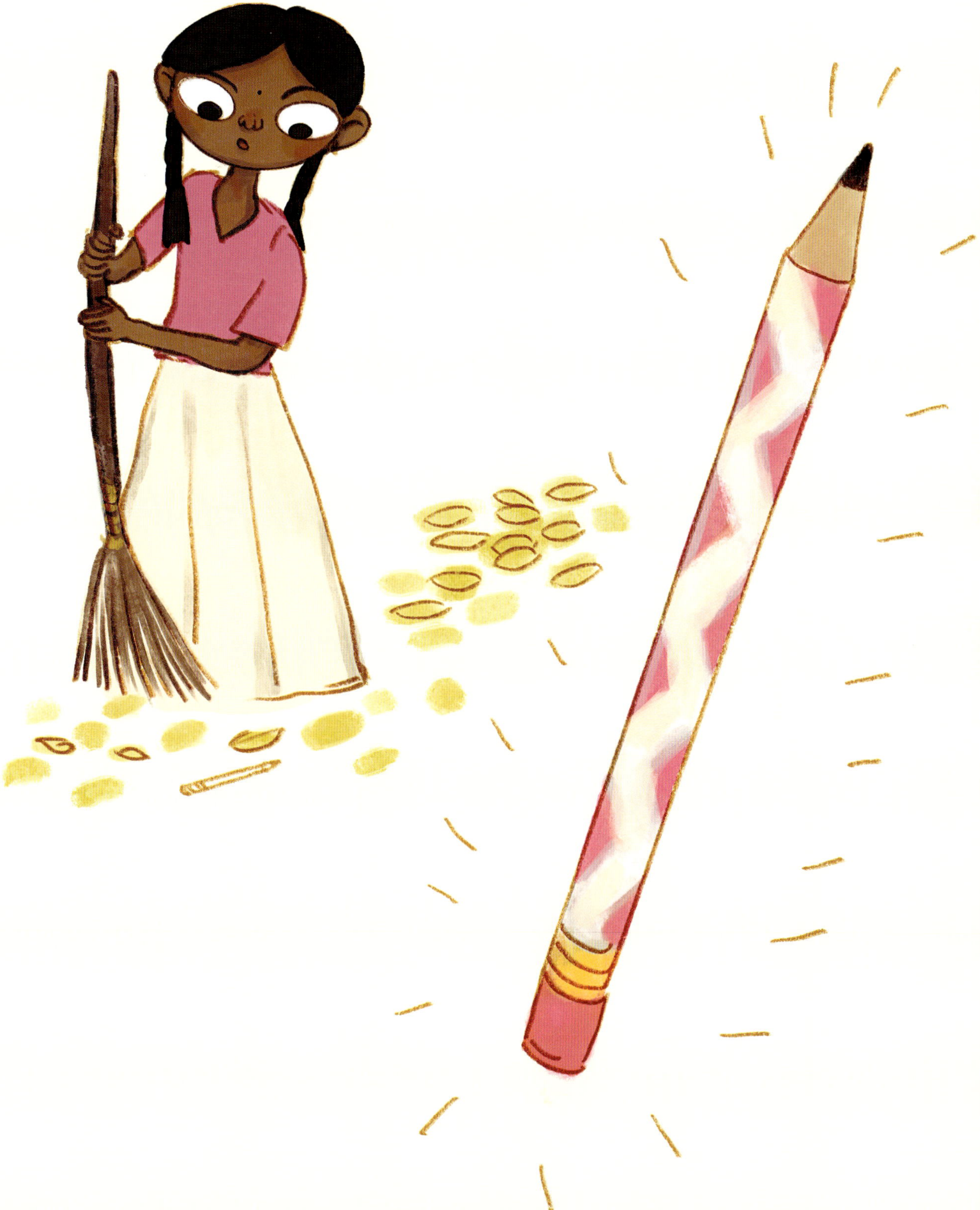

Her father was a daily wage worker and didn't have enough money to send her to school. Karthyayani was heartbroken when he said, 'No school for you.'

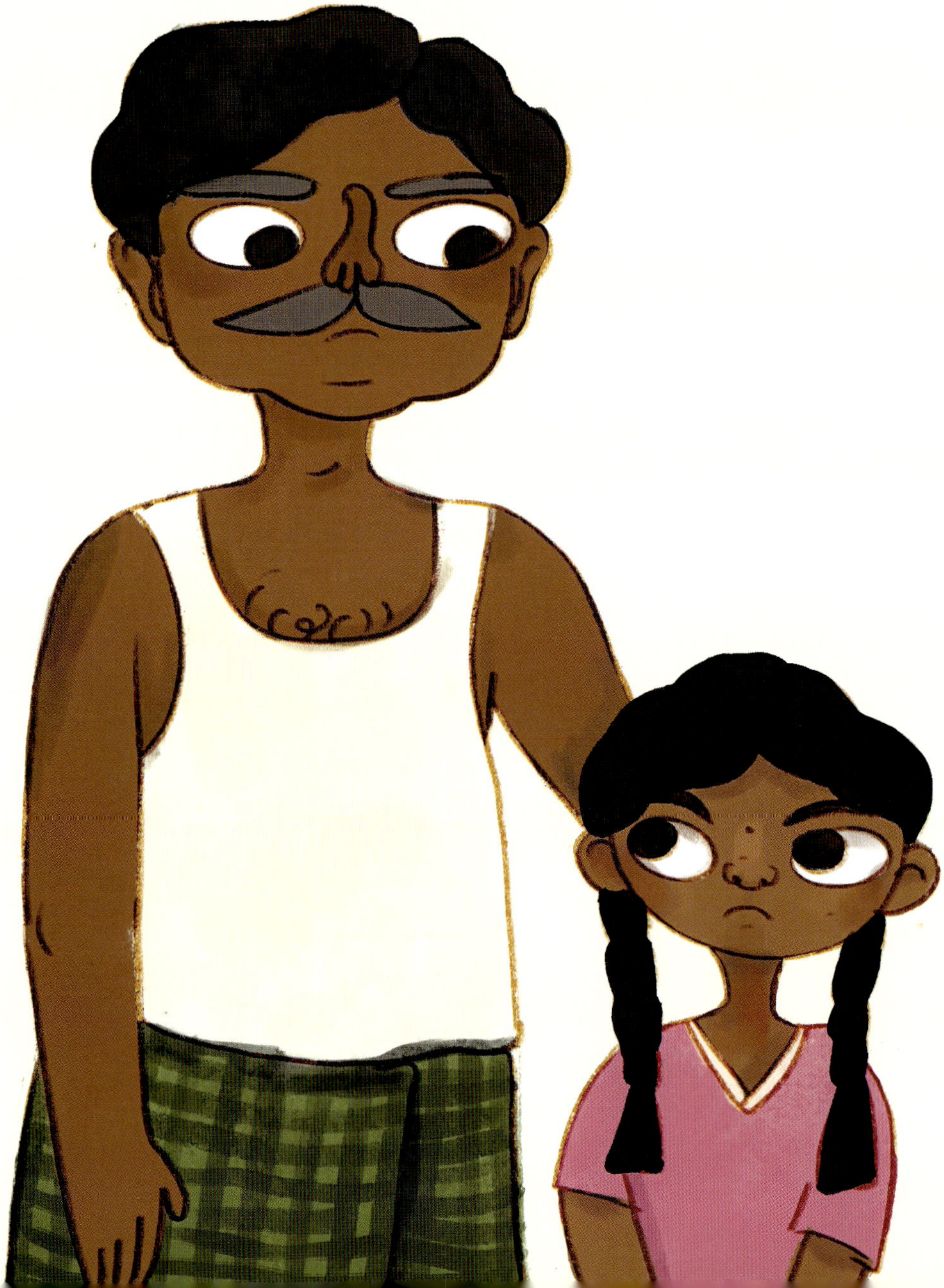

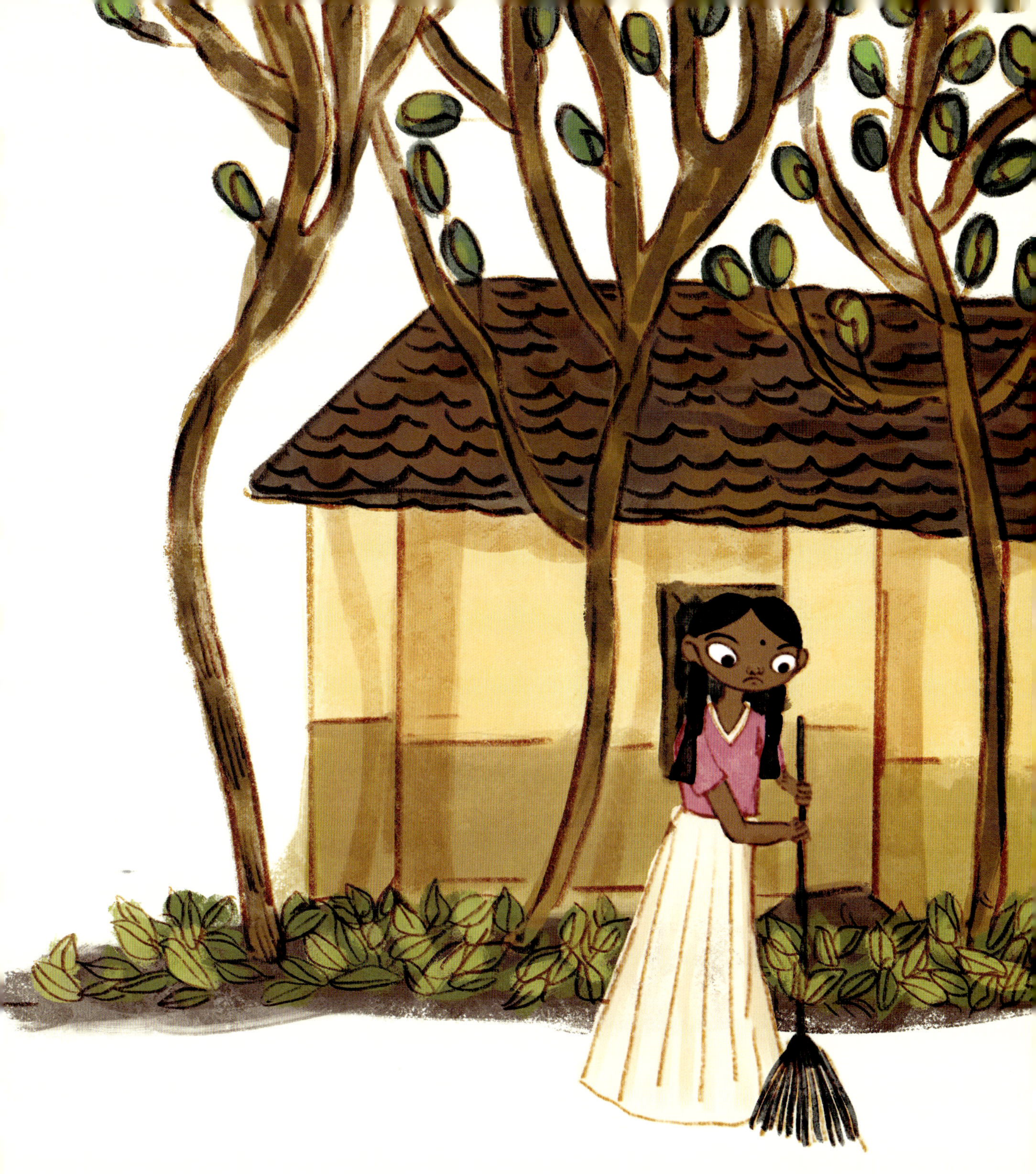

Soon there was even less money at home, and she had to start cleaning the streets to make ends meet.

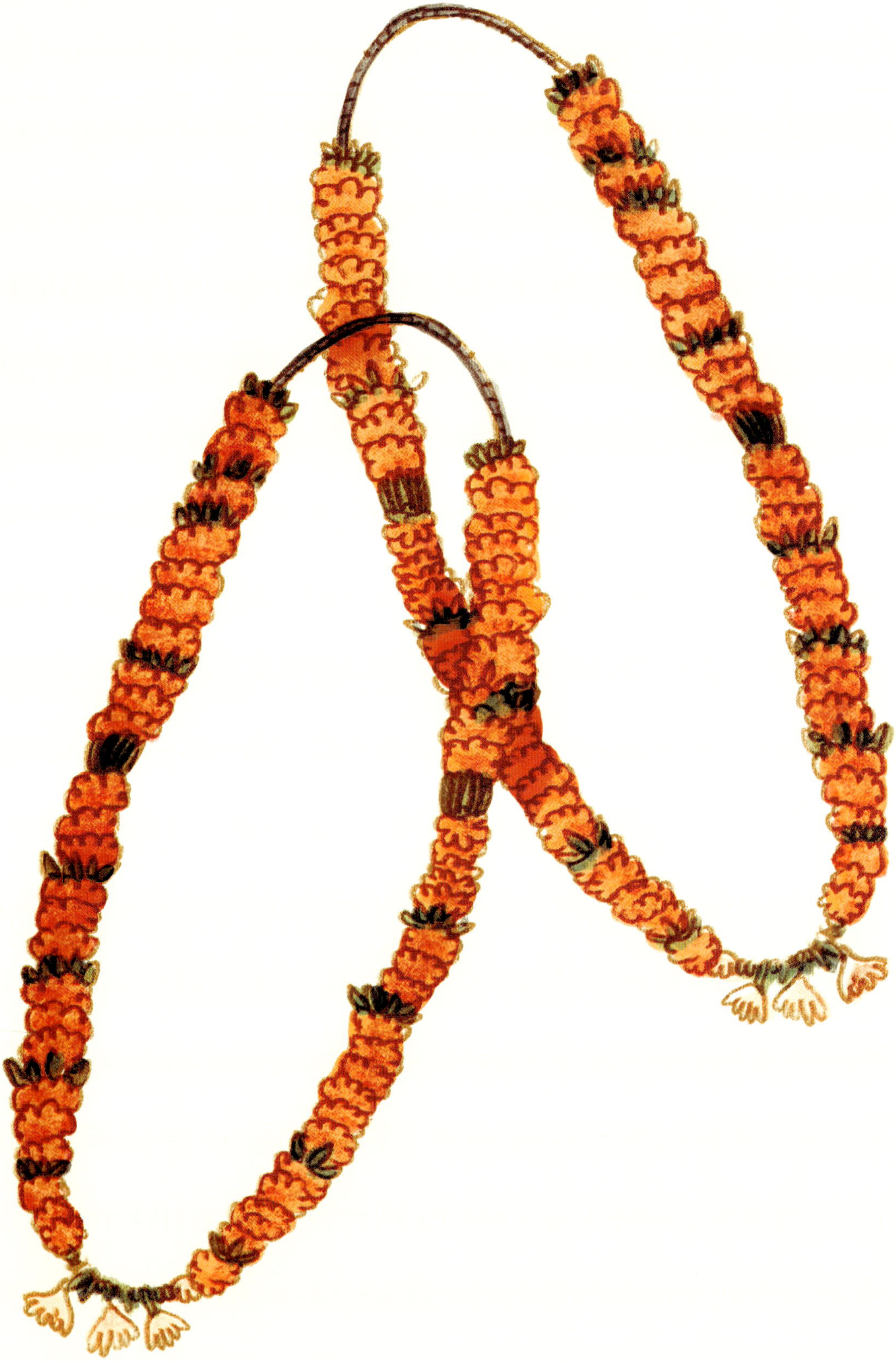

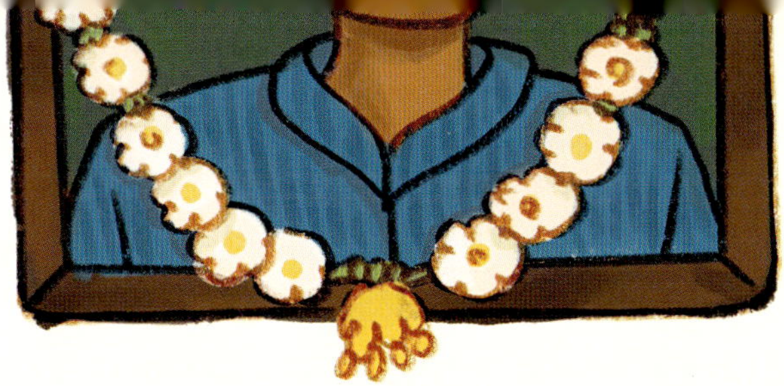

She was married at the age of sixteen and had six children. Then her husband died and she had to bring up the kids on her own. Once again, she started sweeping the streets outside temples.

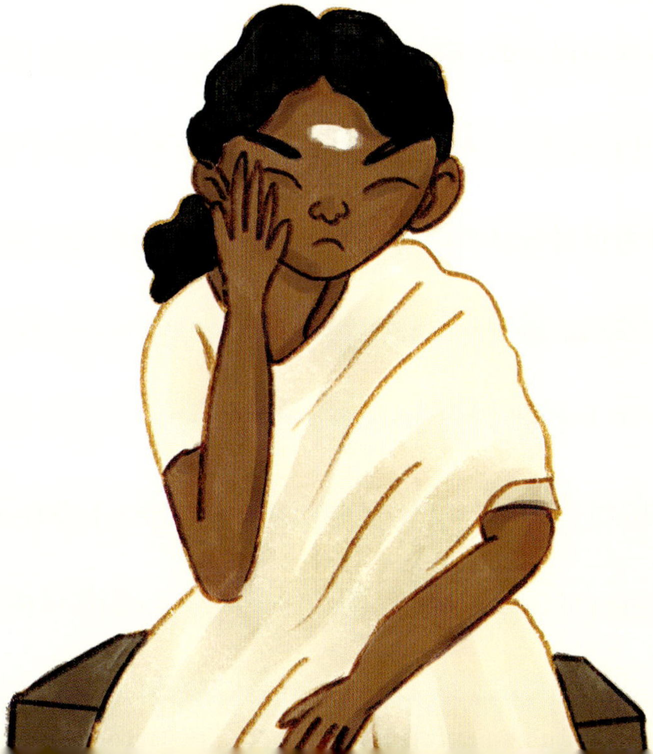

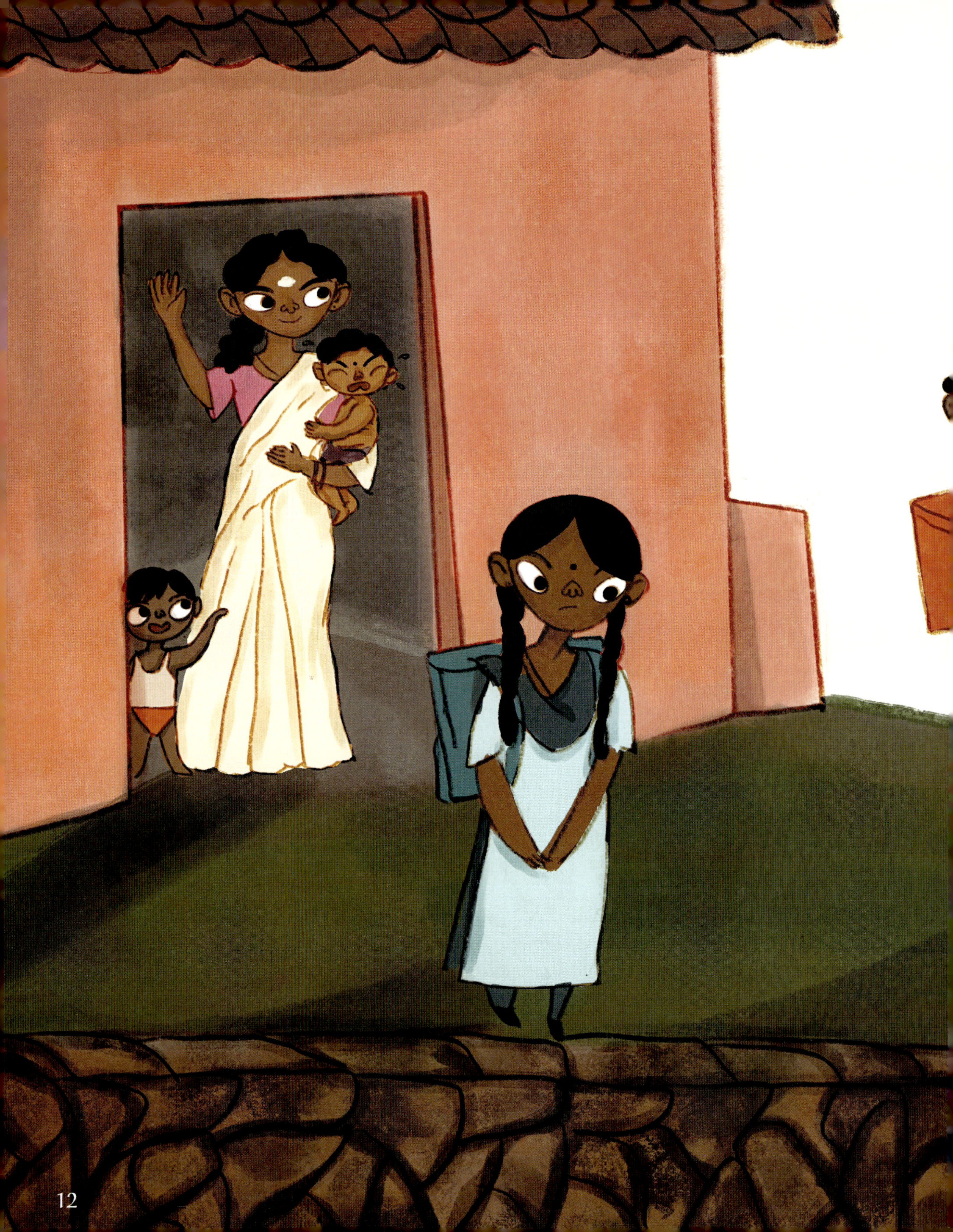

Her children got married and had children. Their children got married and had their own families. As the years went by, Karthyayani got old and wrinkled and her back began to bend.

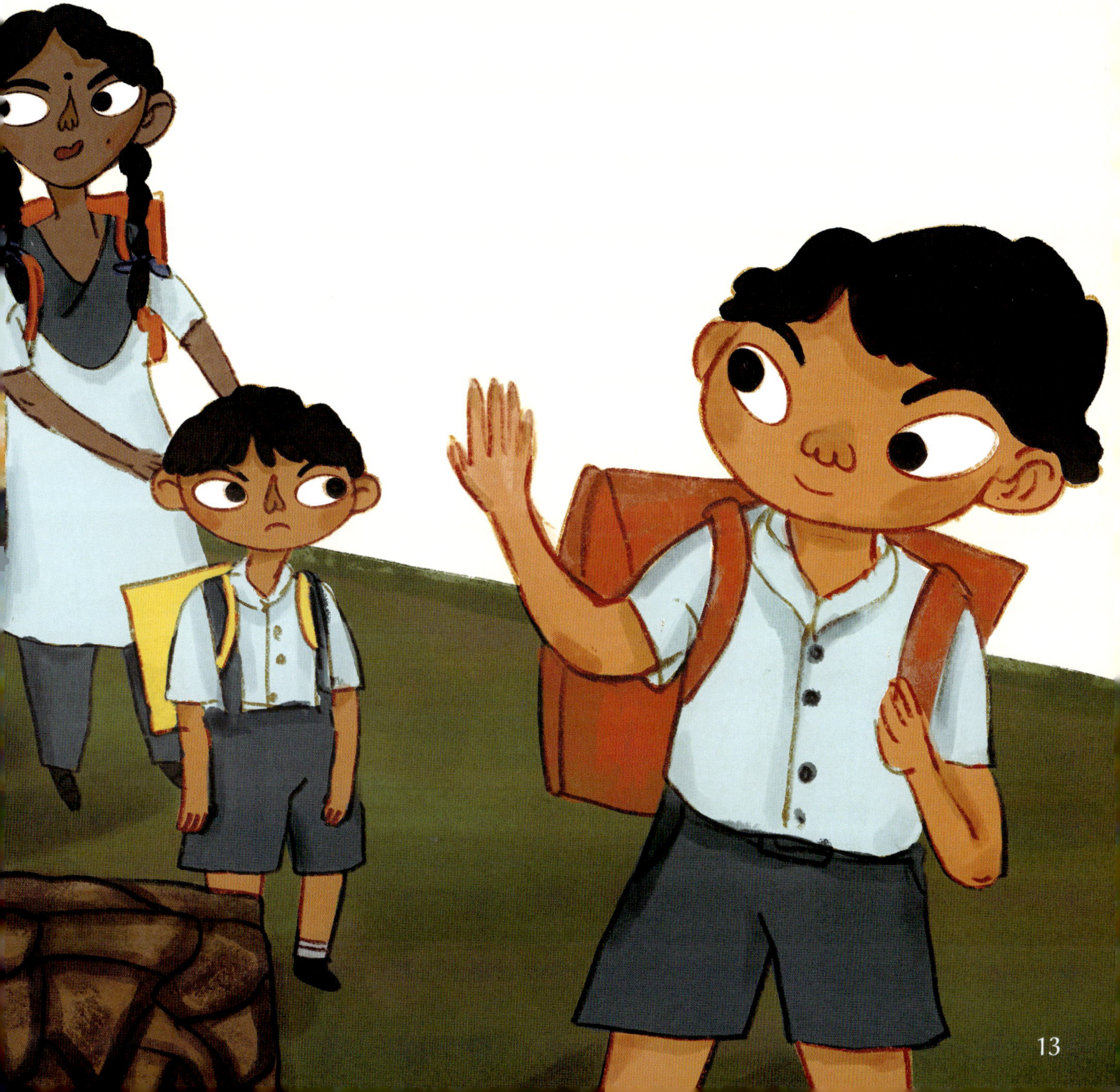

Karthyayani felt life was hard and that she did not get any respect for her work. But she had to earn to feed her children and send them to school.

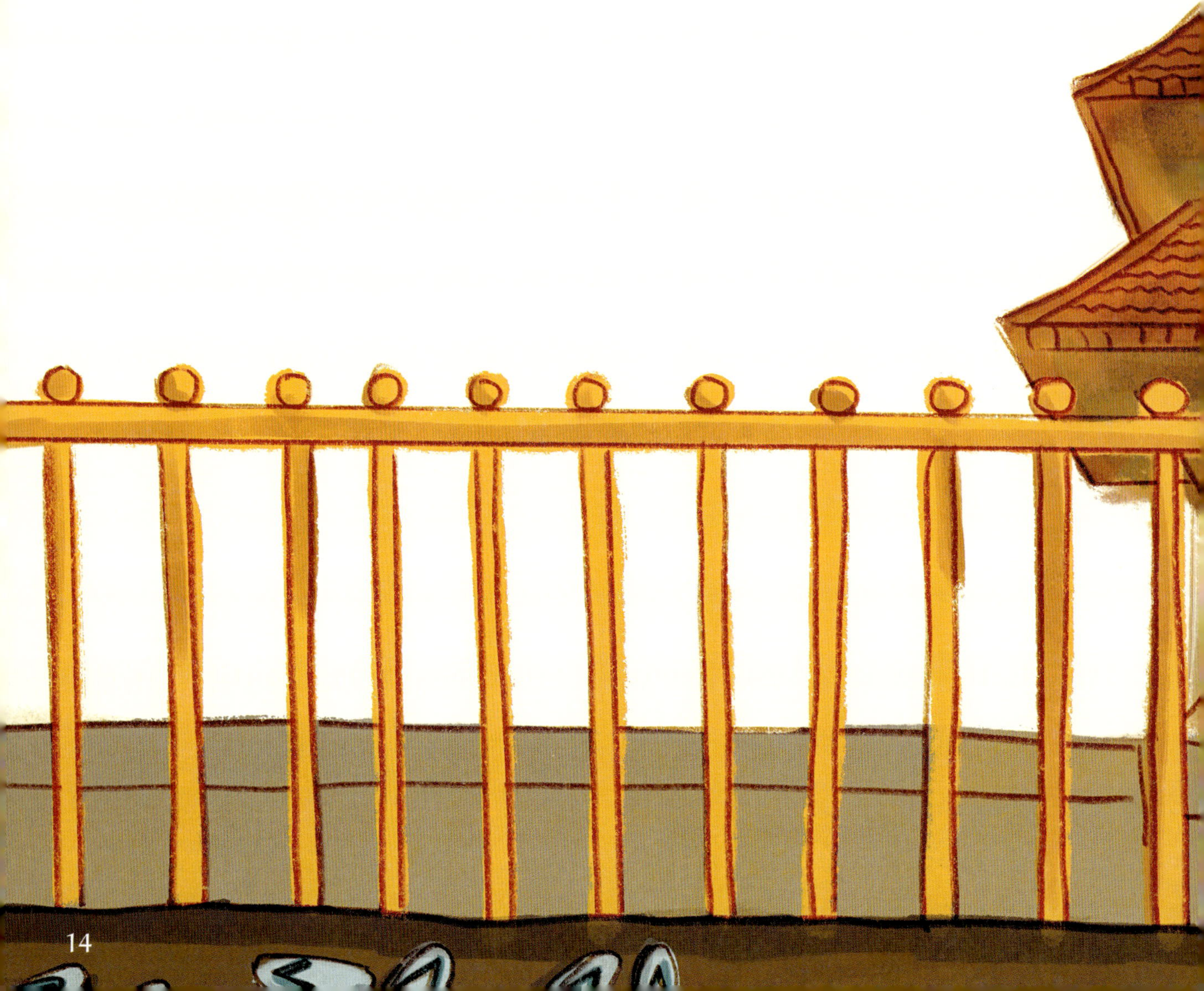

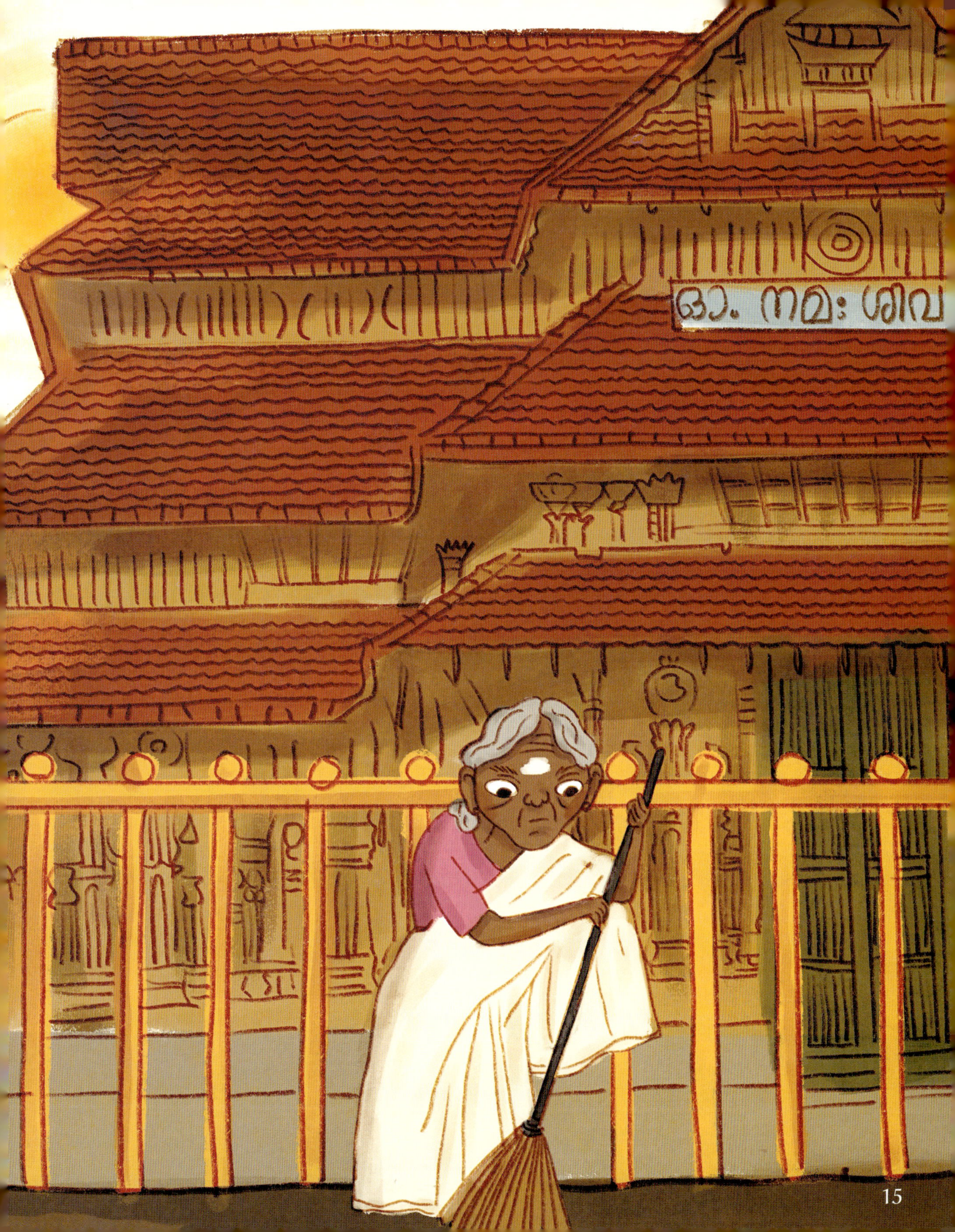
ഓം നമഃ ശിവ

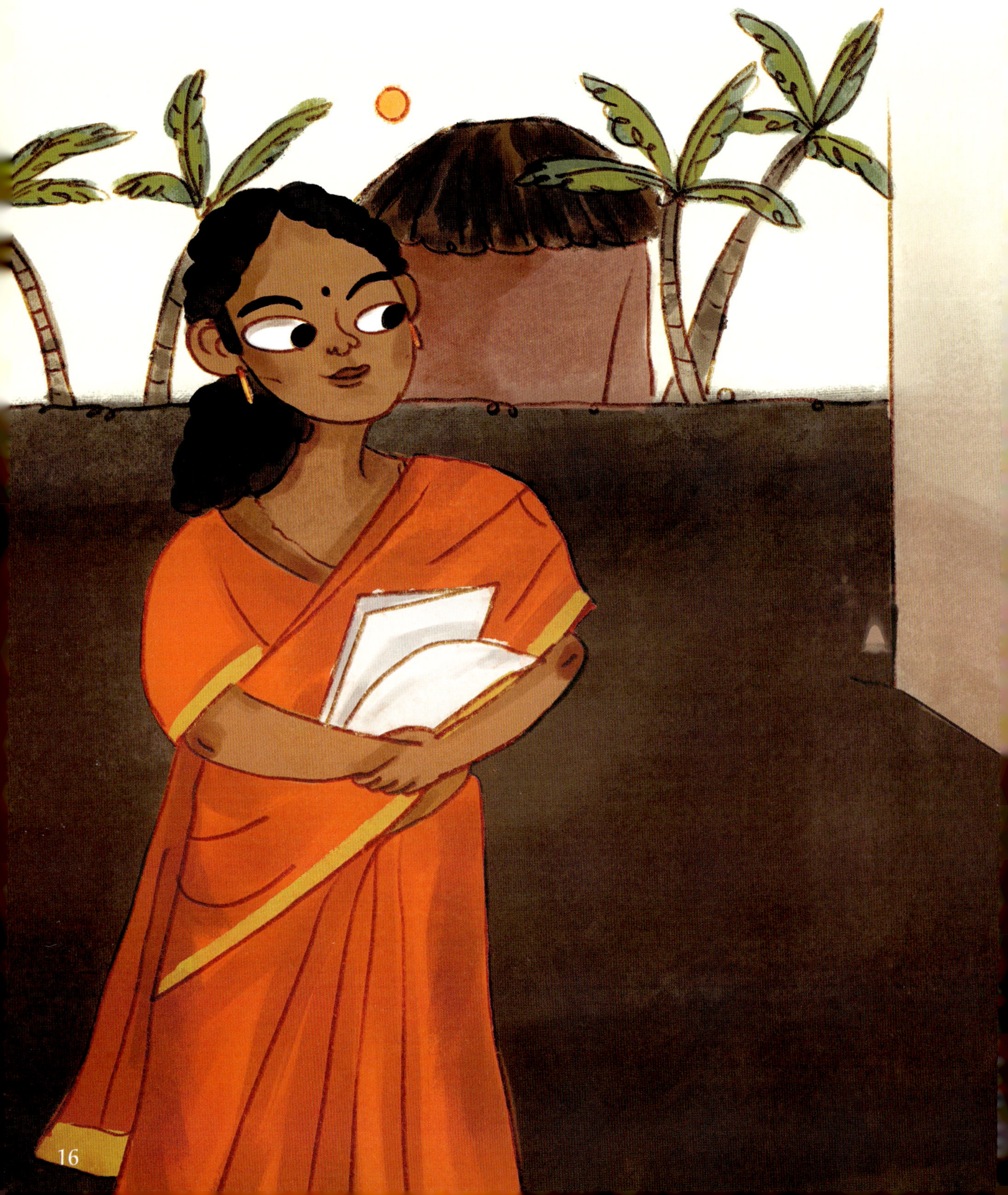

One day, when Karthyayani was ninety-six, she was sitting outside her house when a woman passed by.

The woman, Sathi, said she was an educationist. She was doing a survey to see how many children in the village did not go to school. She asked Karthyayani if there were any in her house.

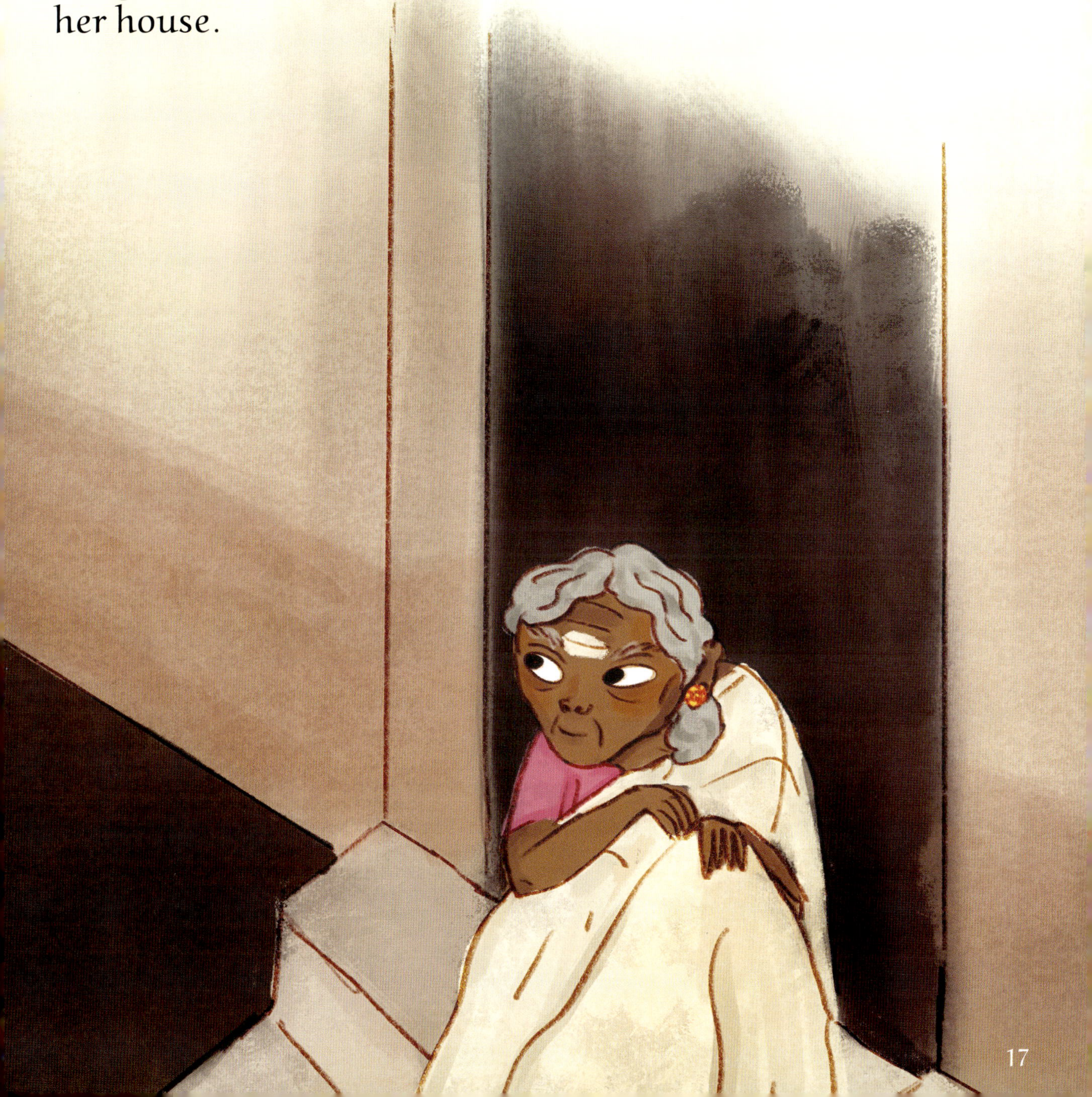

Karthyayani said, 'I'm the only one.' Sathi smiled but Karthyayani was serious.

She said, 'I'm ready to study if you are ready to teach me.'

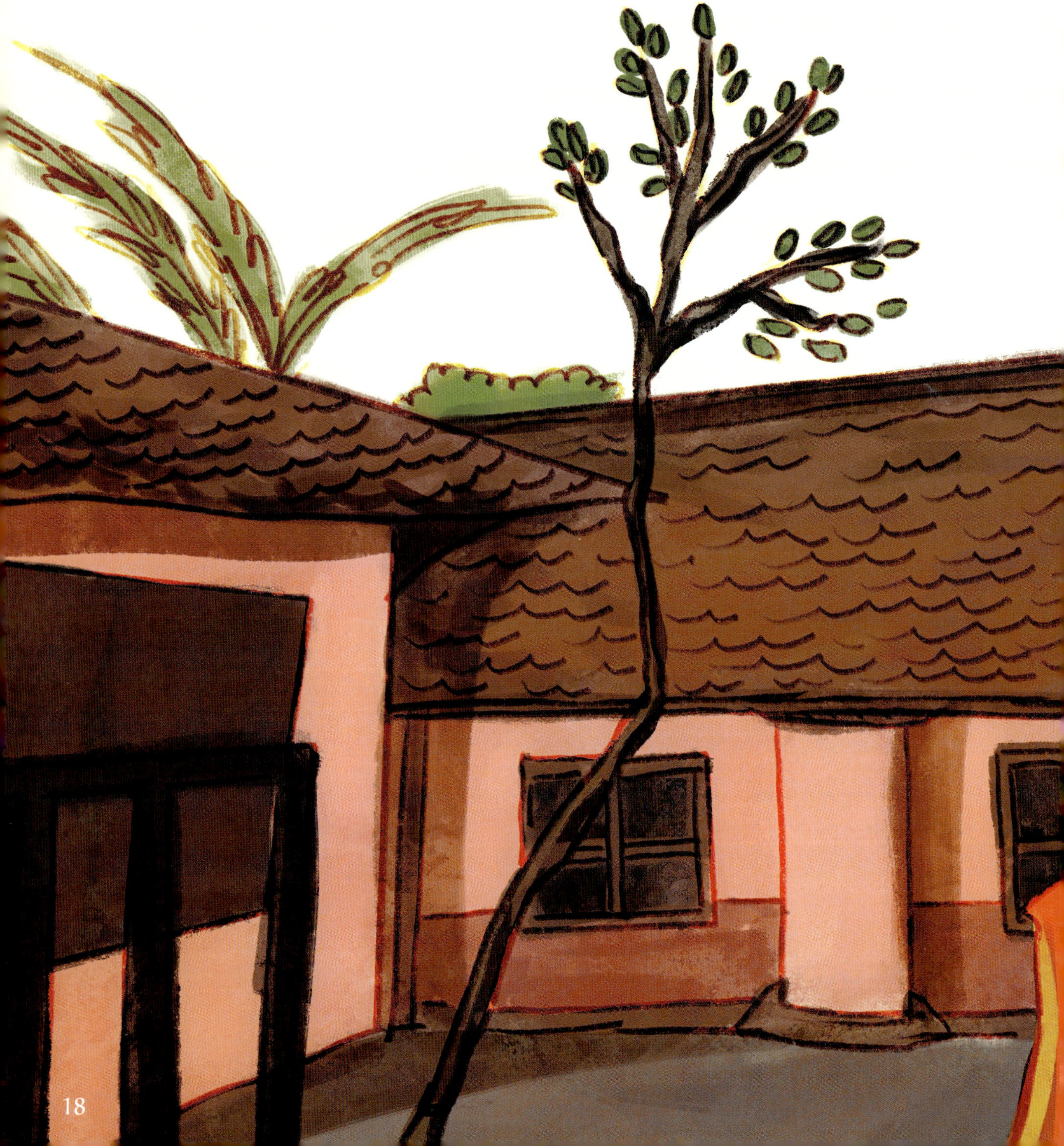

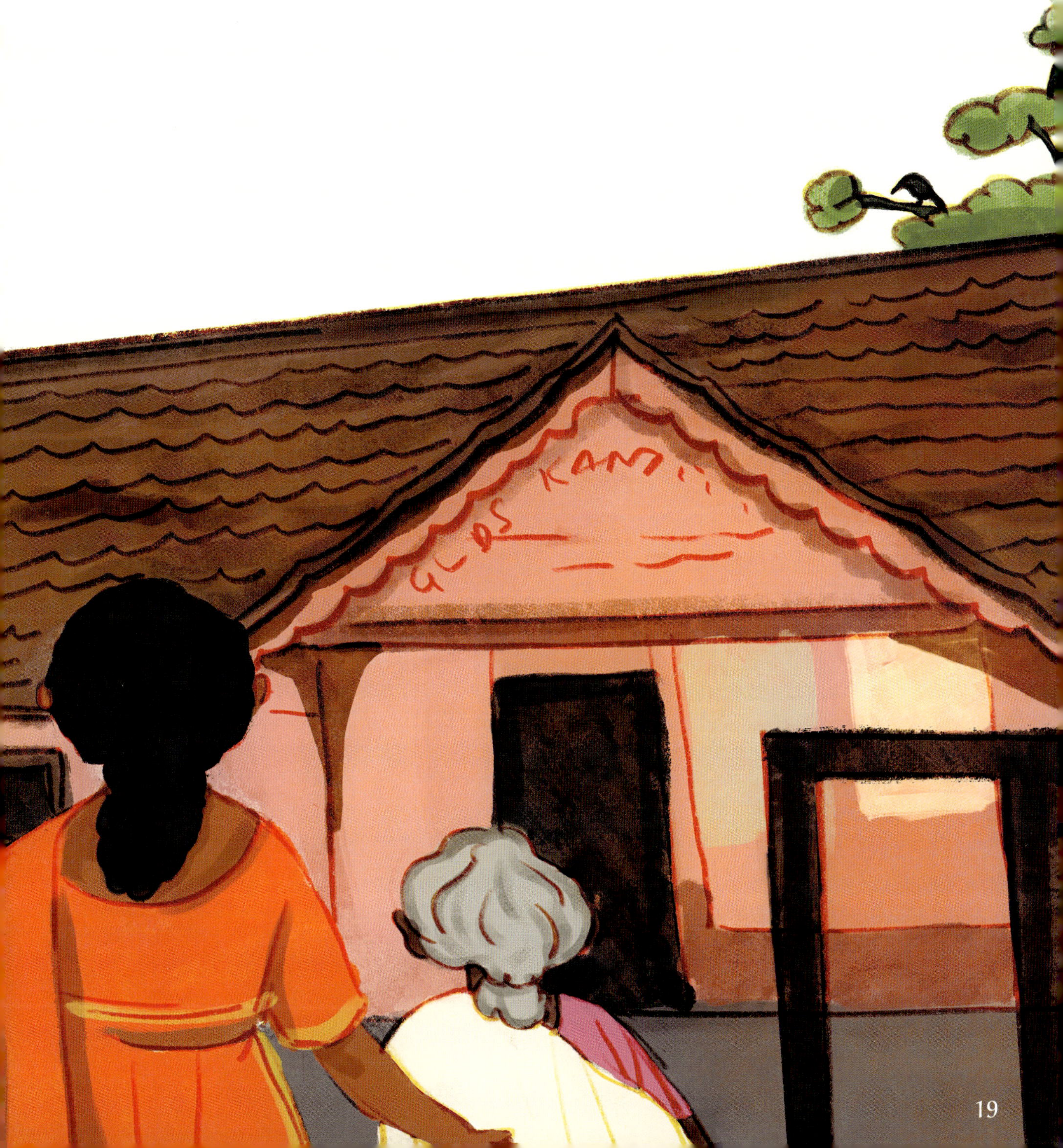

Karthyayani joined a nearby school. Some of her classmates were as young as her great-grandchildren. Some of them laughed at her—she was so old and did not know how to read. Some of the people in the village too made fun of her.

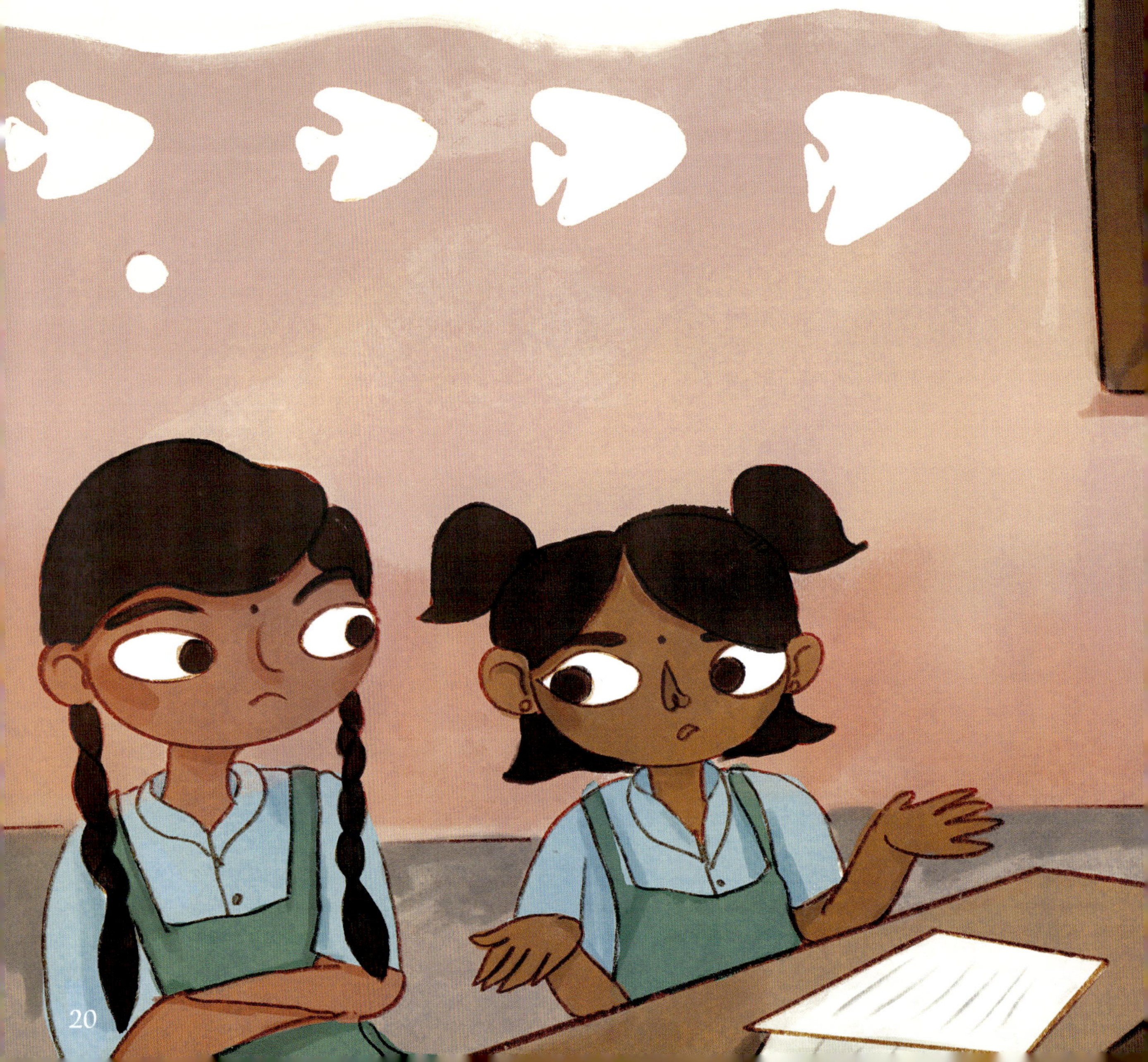

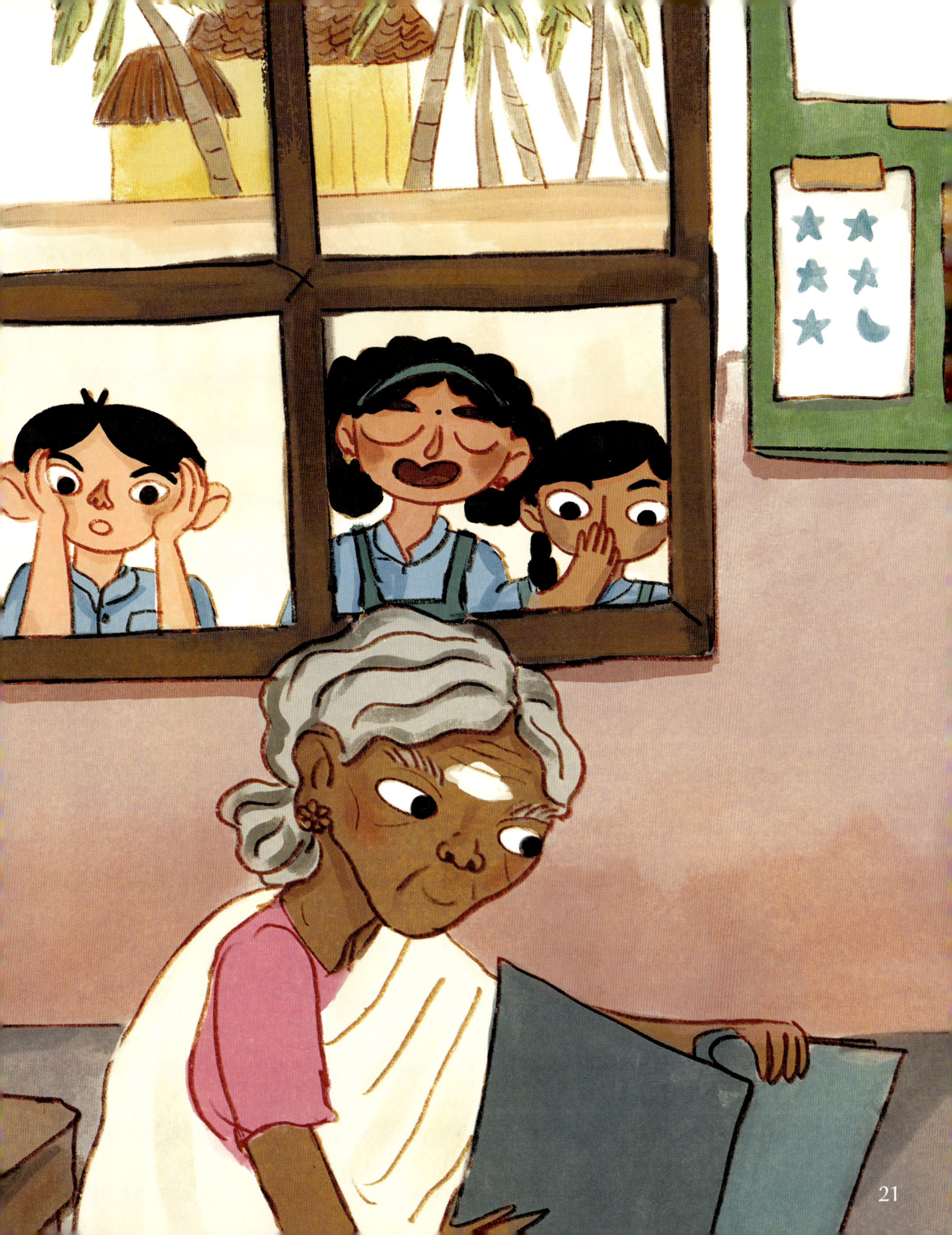

But Karthyayani was not put off. She felt very different from the students in her class. But she was determined to learn and studied hard.

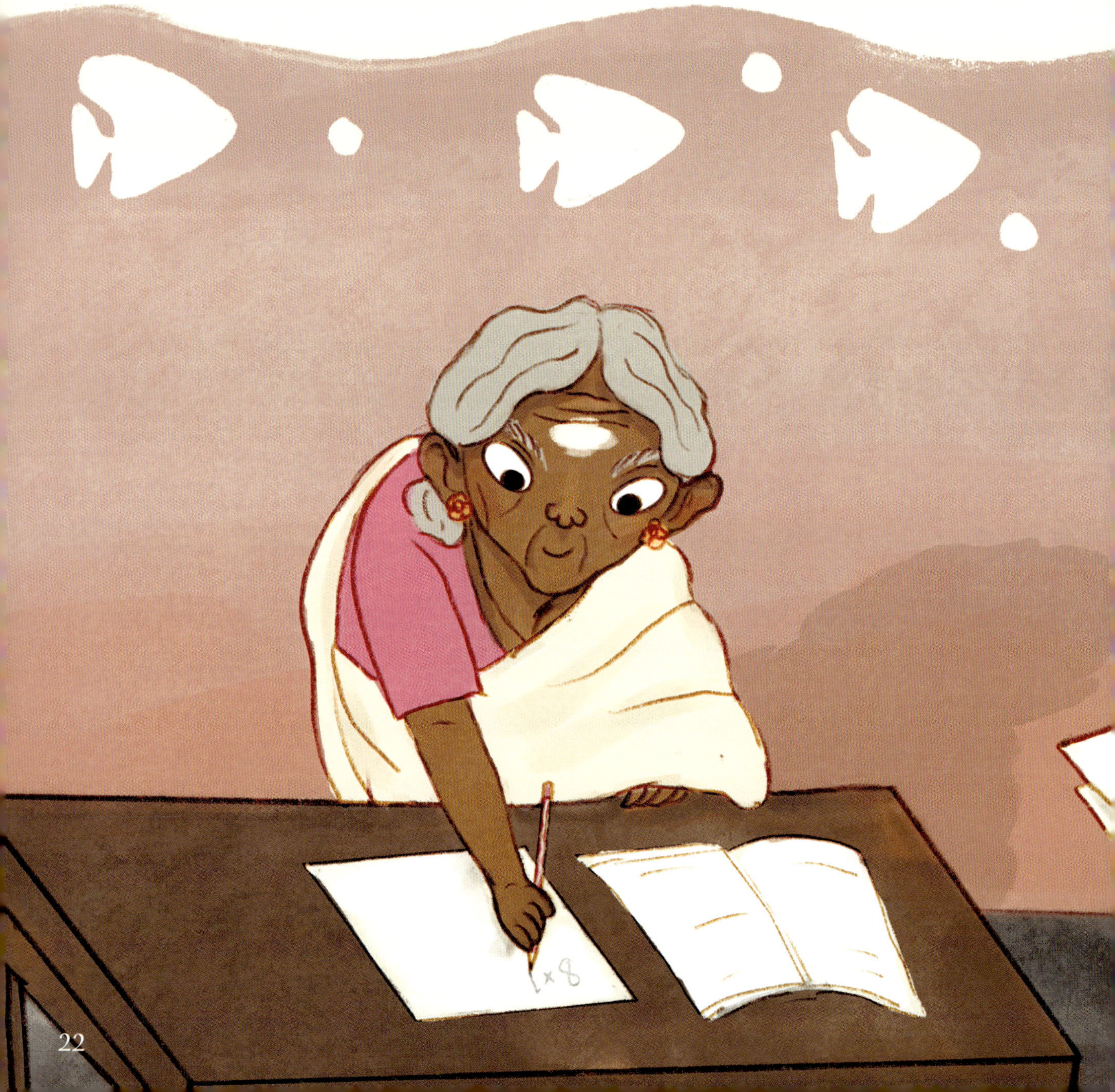

Soon, the little girls in her class were so impressed by how much she wanted to learn that they became friends with her.

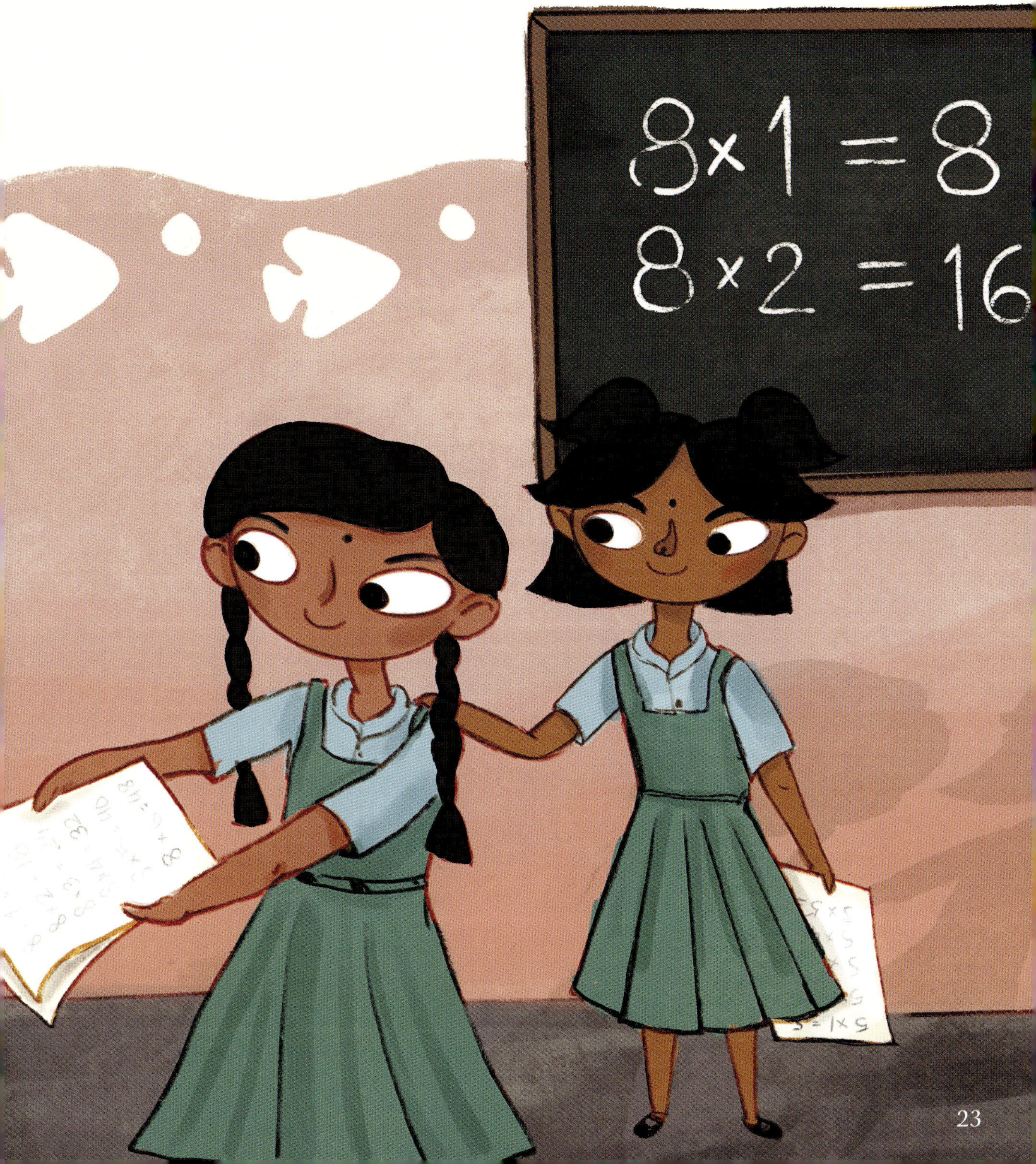

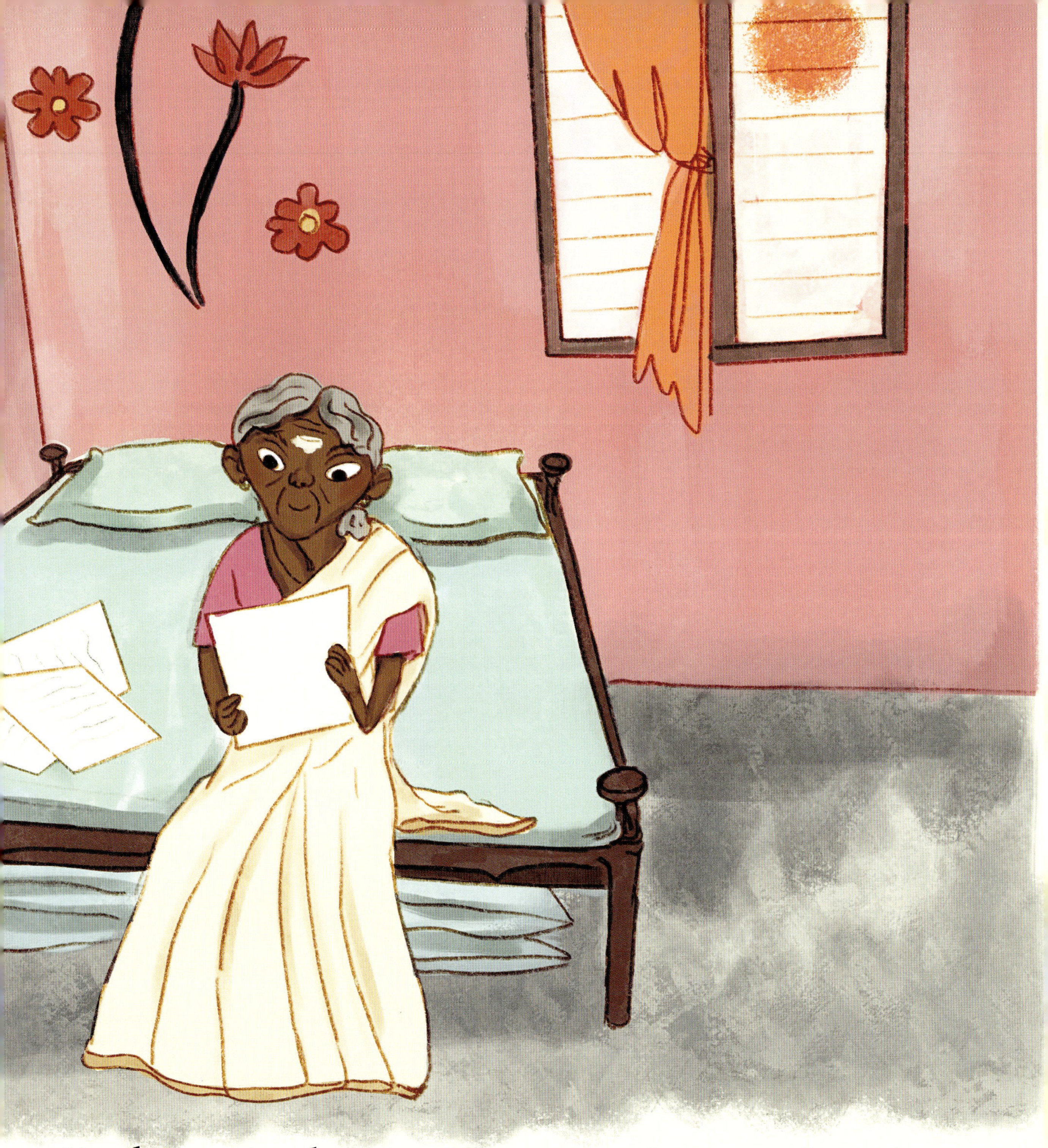

Karthyayani woke up at 3 a.m. every day to study and complete her homework. All the teachers and students were surprised by her determination and hard work.

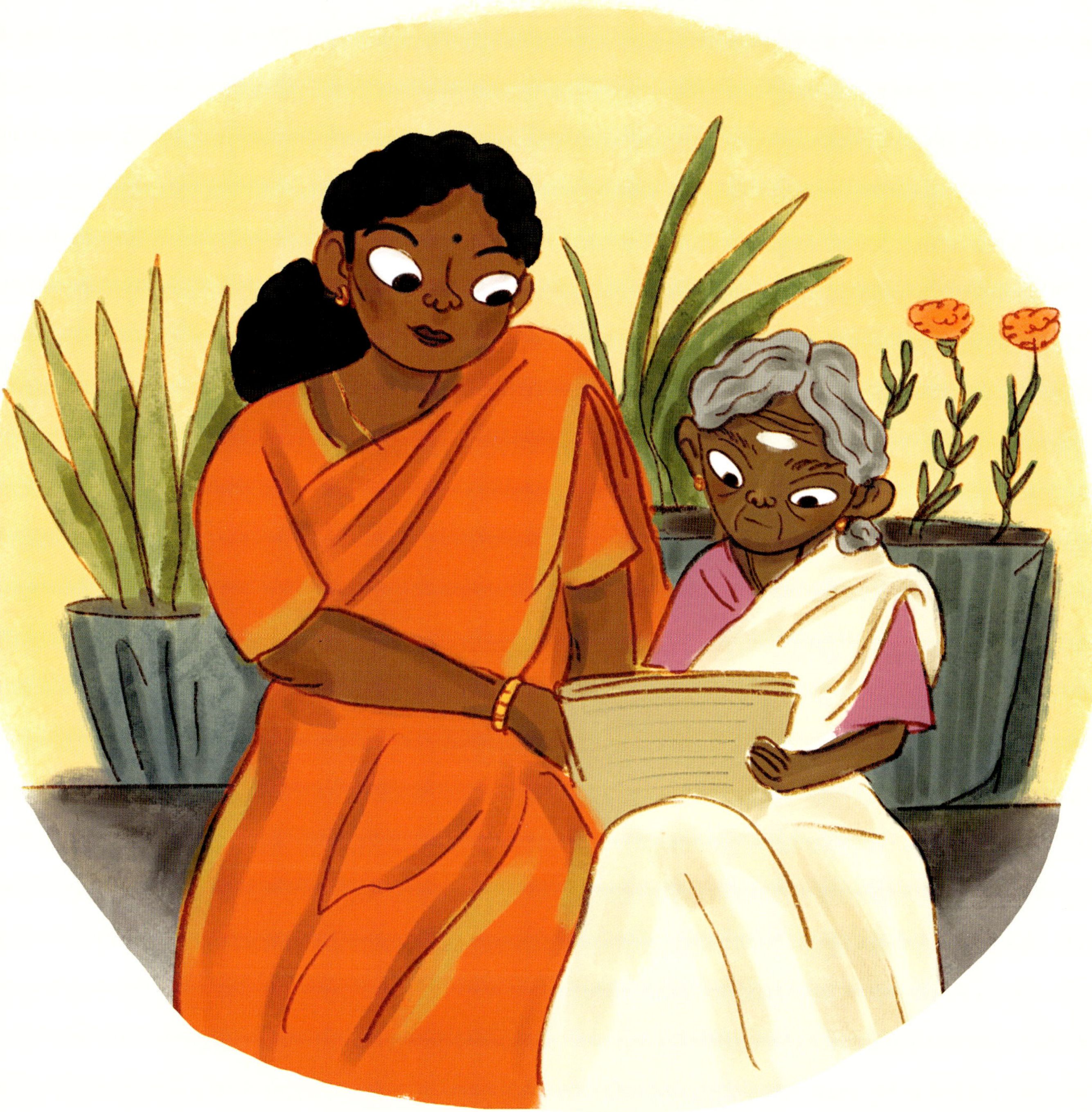

It was time for the final exam. Karthyayani reviewed all her lessons with Sathi, especially mathematics, which she found difficult.

On the day of the exam, she said her prayers and picked up her pink and white pencil and headed to school.

The exam was hard, but she answered all the questions.

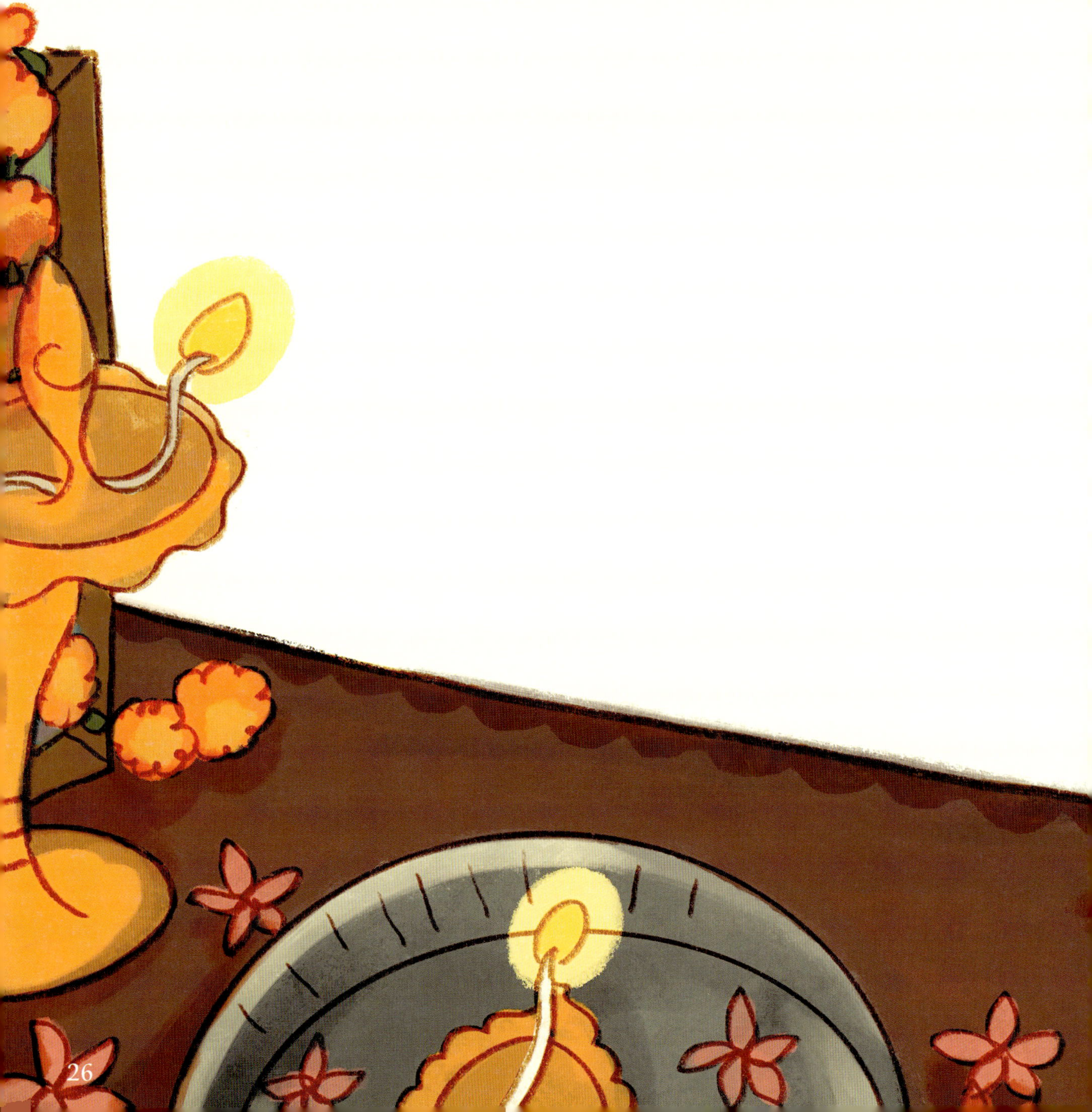

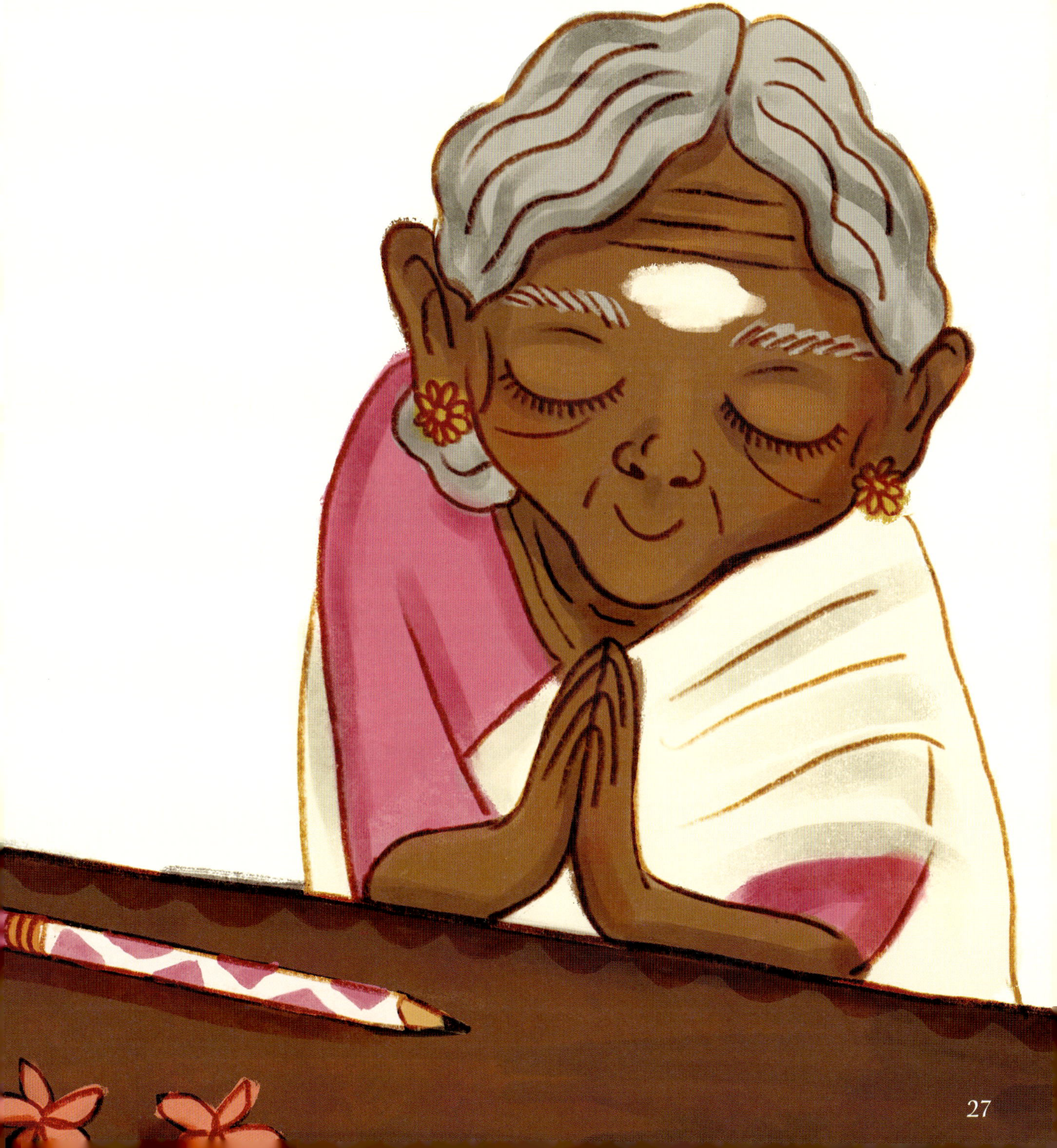

On the day of the prize-giving ceremony for all the schools in the district, everyone was stunned when the person who had scored the highest marks in the state of Kerala and won the top prize turned out to be Karthyayani.

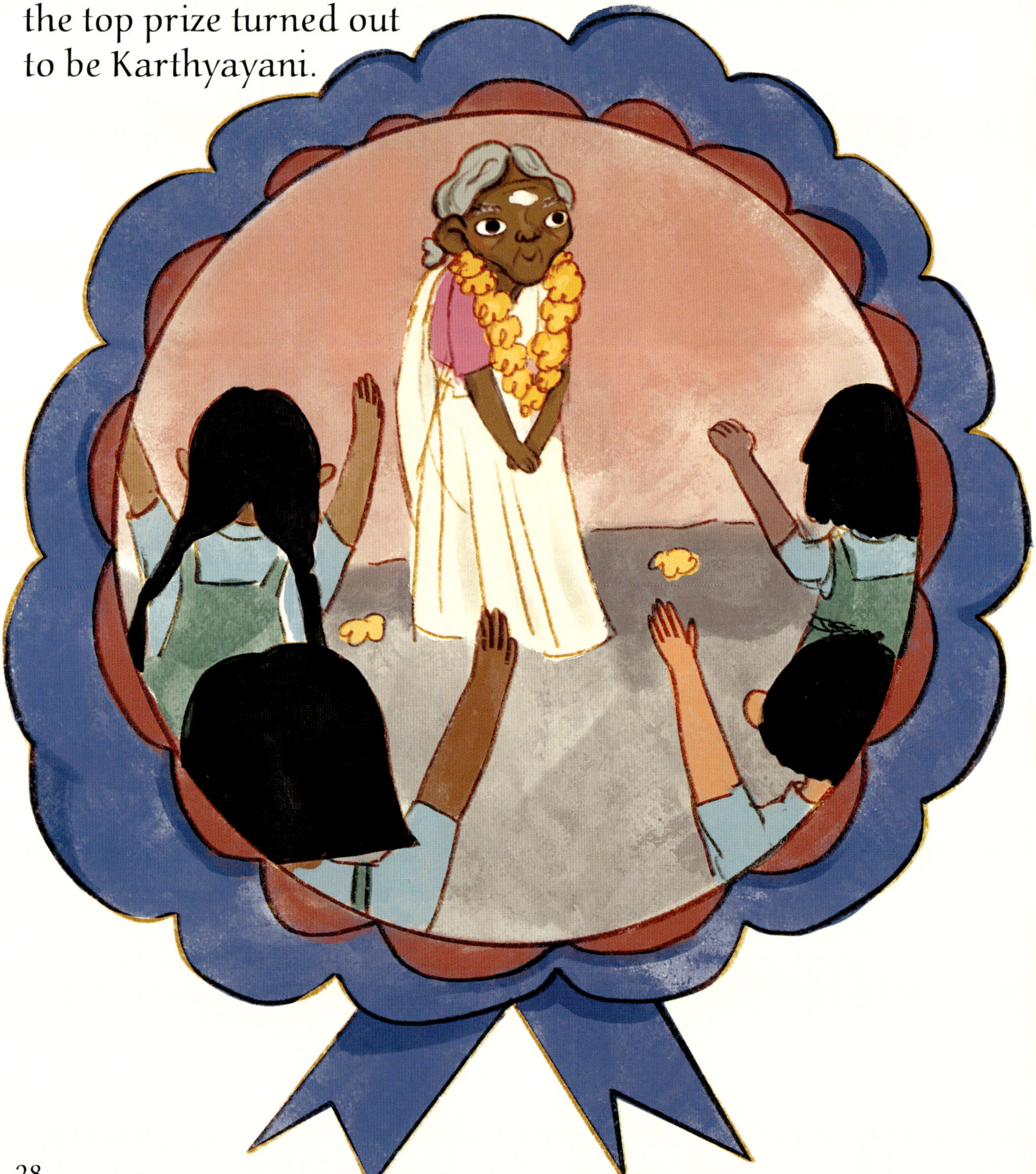

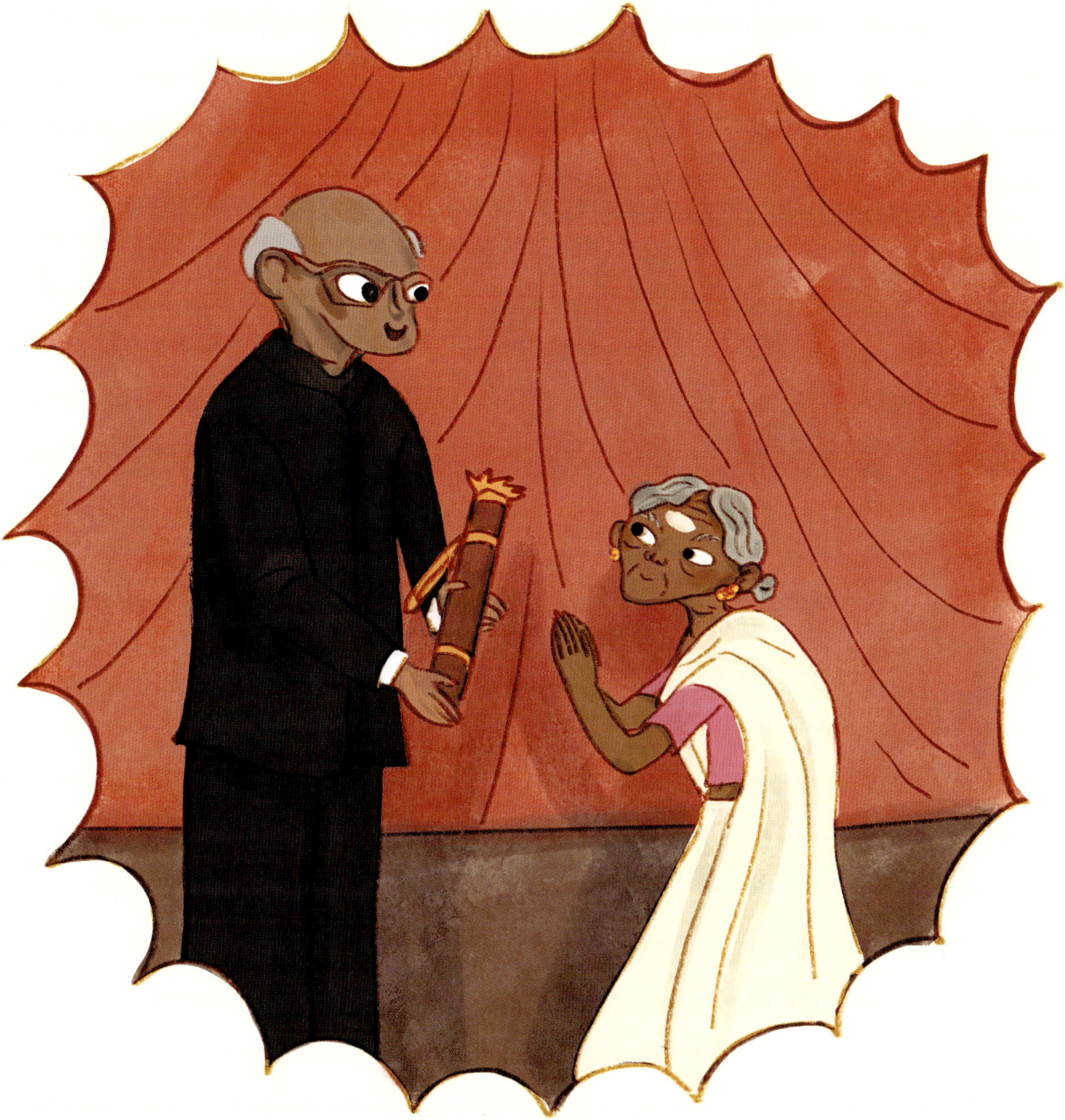

For her incredible achievement, Karthyayani was awarded the Women's Empowerment Award by the President of India. The story of Karthyayani teaches us that you can accomplish your dreams at any age if you are willing to work hard and stay focused.

About Karthyayani Amma

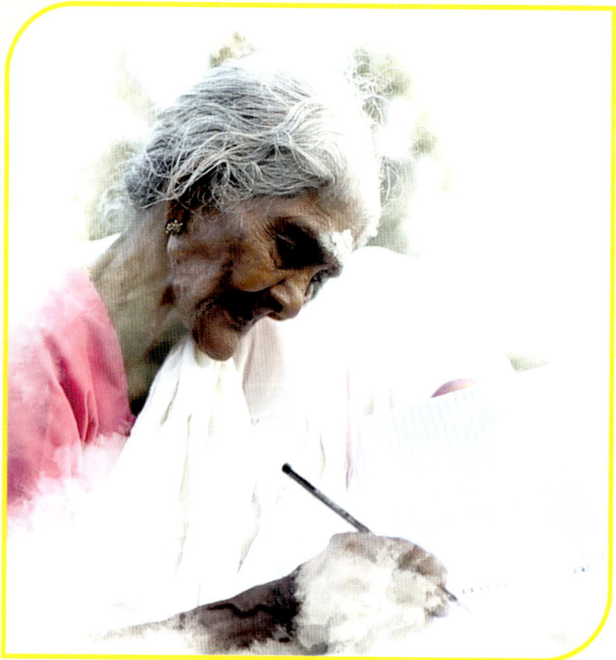

Barefoot Empress revolves around the remarkable journey of Karthyayani Amma, who, having never had access to education as a girl, finally gets a chance to study. At 96 years she was the oldest among the 43,330 candidates who appeared for the 'Aksharalaksham' test. Karthyayani Amma surprised the entire country by topping the literacy examination conducted by the Kerala government, scoring a stellar 98 out of 100. The state-run Kerala State Literacy Mission Authority (KSLMA) has certified that her score is a record.

Karthyayani Amma, who hails from Haripad in the Alappuzha district, swept the streets outside temples in her village for a living.

Amma doesn't plan on stopping anytime soon. She plans to complete her Class 10 equivalent when she turns 100. In 2019 she became a Commonwealth of Learning Goodwill Ambassador. She was awarded the Nari Shakti Puraskar by President Ram Nath Kovind on Women's Day in March 2020.

Her inspirational story is proof that it is never too late to realise your dreams.

BLOOMSBURY INDIA
Bloomsbury Publishing India Pvt. Ltd
Second Floor, LSC Building No. 4
DDA Complex, Pocket C – 6 & 7
Vasant Kunj, New Delhi 110070

BLOOMSBURY, BLOOMSBURY INDIA and the Diana logo are trademarks of Bloomsbury Publishing Plc

First published 2022

ISBN: 978-93-56402-38-6
2 4 6 8 10 9 7 5 3 1

Printed and bound in India by Thomson Press India Ltd

Bloomsbury Publishing Plc makes every effort to ensure that the papers used in the manufacture of our books are natural, recyclable products made from wood grown in well-managed forests. Our manufacturing processes conform to the environmental regulations of the country of origin

To find out more about our authors and books visit www.bloomsbury.com and sign up for our newsletters

Also by VIKAS KHANNA

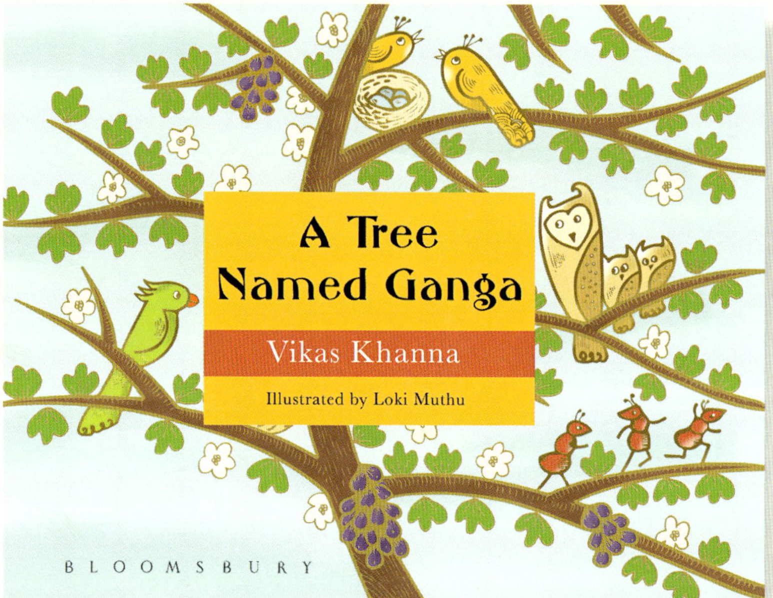

A Tree Named Ganga is the story of a seed that grows into a majestic tree with everyone's love and support. One day, she loses all her friends due to her arrogance.

That is when she learns the greatest lesson of life